OWLS!

STRANGE AND WONDERFUL

Laurence Pringle   Illustrated by Meryl Henderson

BOYDS MILLS PRESS
AN IMPRINT OF HIGHLIGHTS
Honesdale, Pennsylvania

To David Reuther, a steadfast friend and an editor with
rare compassion, sensibility, and wisdom
—LP

To Mary Ann Asciutto—dear friend and wonderful agent—
many thanks
—MH

Boyds Mills Press
An Imprint of Highlights
815 Church Street
Honesdale, Pennsylvania 18431
boydsmillspress.com
Printed in Malaysia

ISBN: 978-1-62091-651-3
Library of Congress Control Number: 2015946893

First edition
Production by Sue Cole
The text is set in Goudy Oldstyle.
The illustrations are done in watercolor and pencil.

10 9 8 7 6 5 4 3 2 1

They are called ghost birds.

They hunt in the night.

They fly with silent wings, and swoop down to pounce on prey with sharp claws.

They call with hisses, howls, wails, yowls, or screams that may send a shiver of fear down your spine.

They are owls.

*Ural owl of Europe
and Northern Asia*

Owls live on every continent except Antarctica. You can find them just about anywhere—in the tropics, Arctic **tundra**, forests, plains, deserts, suburbs, and even in the neighborhoods and parks of some cities. They are appealing, popular birds. People love their faces, their big eyes, and even their spooky calls. But many kinds of owls are active only at night, and are seldom seen. They are birds of mystery.

Throughout history, owls have inspired superstitions, myths, and legends. An Inuit tale explains how the first owl was created. By magic, a young girl was changed into a bird with a long beak. Frightened by this sudden change, she started to fly frantically. She flew face-first into a wall! Her face and beak were flattened. She became an owl.

Ancient Greek coins

Athena

People once believed that owls were evil omens of death. In Central America, the Mayan god of death, Ah-Puch, wore an owl mask as a disguise. In North America, many native tribes feared owls. A child who misbehaved might have been warned, "The owls will get you!" Even today, a West African word for "owl" means "witchbird."

In contrast, the Oglala Sioux of the North American plains believed that men who wore owl feathers had improved eyesight—an aid in hunting and in battle. In other places around the world, some people thought that owls brought good luck and were very wise. Athena, the Greek goddess of wisdom, was often depicted with an owl nearby. To this day, wise owls appear in stories for children. Owls are vital messengers between characters in the Harry Potter series. (Harry's was a snowy owl named Hedwig.)

Ah-Puch

Medieval jousting shield

Northern spotted owl

Northern hawk owl

Burrowing owls

There are about 240 kinds, or species, of owls on Earth. Each species makes distinctive calls. Very few owls "hoot," but they produce an amazing variety of other sounds. Males do most of the calling, and females usually make different sounds.

Owl species also vary by the places they live (their **habitat**), and the prey they hunt. Many species of owls live in forests. They often rely on a keen sense of hearing to detect mice and other animals to catch. Other kinds of owls live in open country. They usually search for prey by sight in daylight.

While many owls rest and nest in trees, and others do so on the ground, one species raises its young underground. The burrowing owl prefers to use abandoned mammal dens, or other tunnel-like holes. They sometimes enlarge the burrows by digging with their beaks and feet.

Different owl species also have differently shaped heads. The tops of their heads are either flat or rounded. Some species have feathered tufts that are easily mistaken for ears. These tufts can help owls hide. When an owl raises its "ears," pulls its feathers tight to its body, and closes its eyes, it looks like a branch or tree stub in a forest. An owl can also use these tufts to express its mood. By moving its tufts and face feathers, it can make itself appear either friendly or aggressive to other owls or other animals.

Screech owl

*Scientists who study birds (**ornithologists**) try to understand how different groups are related. They once thought that owls were relatives of hawks. Now they believe owls' closest relatives are a group of birds called goatsuckers. These birds fly at night, catching insects in the air, and include whip-poor-wills, nightjars, and nighthawks (which are not hawks).*

The illustrations in this book show a variety of the world's owls, including the smallest and the biggest, which are shown on these pages.

Elf owl

The elf owl is the smallest of Earth's owls. Smaller than a robin and weighing less than two ounces, it lives in Mexican deserts, and also in southern parts of California, Arizona, New Mexico, and Texas. This tiny owl eats insects and other small prey, including scorpions. Before swallowing a scorpion, the elf owl breaks off its poisonous stinger.

Two species are tied for the title of world's biggest owl. Both can weigh as much as nine pounds and have a wingspan of well over five feet. The Eurasian eagle owl has a huge range. It lives in much of Europe, Central Asia, the Middle East, China, and northern Japan. It hunts from dusk to dawn, often catching sleeping birds by surprise. Its prey includes other kinds of owls and small rodents, but also large hares and even young deer.

Eurasion eagle owl

Blakiston's fish owl

Equally large, Blakiston's fish owl hunts from low perches along rivers and rocky shores. It swoops down to snatch fish from the water. It can snag a salmon that is more than twice its own weight. One of Earth's rarest owls, it survives only in parts of Japan and eastern Russia. Owls that fish do not need silent flight to surprise their prey. Their wing feathers do not muffle sounds as well as those of owls that hunt birds and mammals.

9

Some well-known and widespread owl species are shown here.

The deep *hoo-hoodoo-hooo-hoo* call of male great horned owls can be heard in Canada and Alaska, southward through the continental United States, Mexico, Central America, and even parts of far southern South America. This big owl's "horns" are actually large tufts of feathers. Its eyes are some of the biggest of all American owls.

The great gray owl has an unusually big head, and no feathered "ear" tufts. Its face has unusual markings—a pattern of dark-gray concentric circles. It lives in Siberia, Canada, and Alaska, and also in northern parts of the Rocky and Sierra mountains in the United States. Like other owls that live in frigid northern climates, the great gray owl's feather-covered legs, feet, and toes help protect it from the cold. In winter, the great gray owl can hear a meadow **vole** moving beneath snow, then dive and reach into the snow with its long legs to catch it.

The short-eared owl is one of the most widespread bird species on Earth. It nests on the ground in tundra, grasslands, marshes, and other open lands throughout much of the world. It even lives on the Hawaiian Islands, far from other land. The short-eared owl flies low, looking down for mice, other rodents, and small birds.

More than twenty kinds of screech owls live in North and South America. Like all owls, they make a variety of sounds, but despite their name, these owls don't screech! (Screech owls are related to more than forty kinds of **scops owls** that live elsewhere in the world.) In the United States, the western screech owl's main call is a series of short whistles. The eastern species makes a low, trembling whistle that sounds like the soft whinny of a horse. Hunting at night, screech owls catch mice, small snakes, moths, beetles, other big insects, and even earthworms.

11

People who like owls usually have a favorite kind. The two shown here are on many lists of favorites.

The snowy owl is a symbol of the tundra landscape in the Arctic, Greenland, and Siberia. Adult males are almost pure white, while the white feathers of females are flecked with brown or black bars. Strong, swift fliers, snowy owls hunt by day over the vast open tundra. They eat mostly lemmings and other rodents. Every winter, many snowy owls fly south hundreds of miles. These spectacular birds appear on farm fields, beach dunes, the wide grasslands of airports, and other open spaces in southern Canada and the United States. People are thrilled to see these visitors from the north.

Barn owls do live in barns, and also in abandoned buildings, church steeples, bridges, tunnels, and tree hollows. They also use nest boxes built by people. This species has a heart-shaped face and unusually long legs. It lives all over the world, though not in deserts or in very cold places, such as Siberia and the Arctic. It hunts from dusk to dawn over farm fields and other open countryside, listening for mice and other rodents. In some areas, its main prey is meadow voles; in others, it might be gophers or cotton rats. People living near a barn owl nest may hear a strange mix of sounds—barks, hisses, clicks, trills. And they may be startled by long, loud shrieks—sounds that can be mistaken for human screams.

13

All owls have full-feathered bodies. Underneath are owl skeletons. One is shown here. Surprise! It looks quite small. And the small skull doesn't have a flat front like an owl's face.

Southern boobook owl of Australia

Bony eye ring

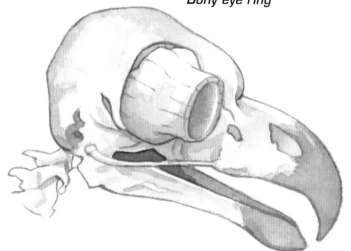

Cutaway view of owl bone

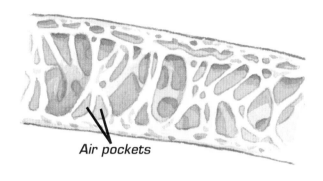

Air pockets

In one way, owl skeletons are like those of other birds. Having lightweight bones makes flying easier, so the bones of all birds are strong but full of air pockets. In other ways, an owl skeleton is suited to how an owl lives. For example, when an owl swoops down to catch prey, it lands hard. Its leg and foot bones are especially stout and strong.

The wing bones shown on this owl skeleton (left) are long, compared to the rest of the body. Owl wings must be large and strong enough to lift and carry the bird and whatever prey it may catch.

The owl's skull has a sharp, hooked beak, space for its brain, and big openings for ears and eyes. Inside each eye is a rigid ring of bones for support. The skull doesn't look much like an owl's flat face, even when covered with muscles and skin. That look is created by several kinds of feathers. And feathers all over can make an owl look big, especially during winter. This is because fluffed-out feathers offer protection from the cold by trapping warmth given off by the owl's body.

One reason people find owls so appealing is simple: they look like us! Owl eyes face forward; so do human eyes. Owl eyelids blink from the top down; so do human eyelids. Nearly all other kinds of birds have eyes on the sides of their heads, and eyelids that blink from the bottom up.

Like you, owls have **binocular vision**. Two eyes, slightly apart and facing forward, help owls judge distance accurately. But unlike human eyes, owl eyes are also tube-shaped, not round, which helps them see faraway objects very clearly. However, owls can't see nearby objects very well. Small owls that catch insects and other small prey use whisker-like feathers to help them find and catch small prey when they are close to it.

Southern white-faced owl of southern Africa

Binocular vision of an owl

Binocular vision of a pigeon

Short-eared owl

Most birds have eyes on the sides of their heads. This enables them to see all around them, even above their heads. However, they cannot easily judge distances because they lack the binocular eyesight of an owl or a person. If a robin or duck wants to know how close or far something is, it either tips its head from side to side, or bobs its head to get different views with one eye.

Owl eyes are big. Those of a snowy owl weigh as much as those of an adult human. They see especially well in dim light. Owl eyes are much more sensitive in low light than those of most birds.

When you look around, you can do it two ways—by moving your eyes, and by moving your head. Owls can't move their eyes. However, they can turn their heads far enough to look everywhere, in a full circle, without moving their bodies. Owls have fourteen neck bones (**vertebrae**), twice as many as humans. This, and other head features, gives owls remarkable head-turning ability. At times, an owl turns its head from side to side so fast it seems to spin in a full circle, but no animal can do that. Also, owls can turn their heads upside down—the best way to see something overhead.

The outer parts of your ears are in plain sight. Owls also have ears on the sides of their heads, just behind their eyes, but the ear openings are hidden by feathers. Some owl species also have a hidden flap of skin by each ear. An owl can move its ear flaps and other face feathers to help receive sounds. Usually one ear hole of an owl is bigger than the other, and/or slightly higher on its head. This affects how sound waves are received by each ear. It helps an owl pinpoint a mouse or other hidden prey that is moving and making sounds.

Owls' faces are also part of their extraordinary hearing system. Their face feathers form a flat disk, like a saucer. This **facial disk** may be made of six or more different kinds of feathers. Some are short and tightly packed, and make a hard surface that helps bounce sound waves to the ears.

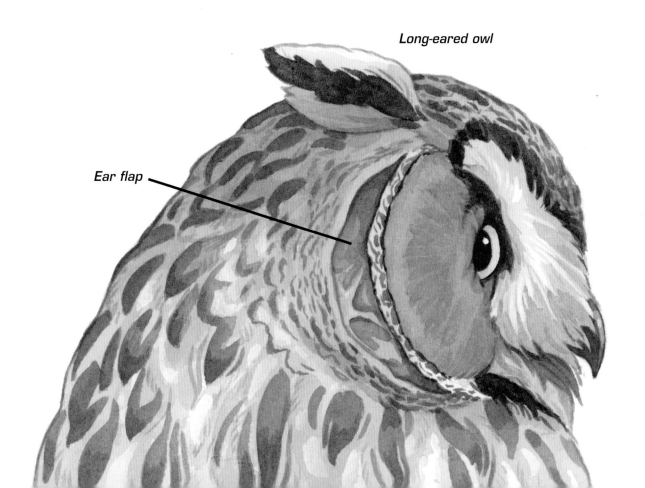

Long-eared owl

Ear flap

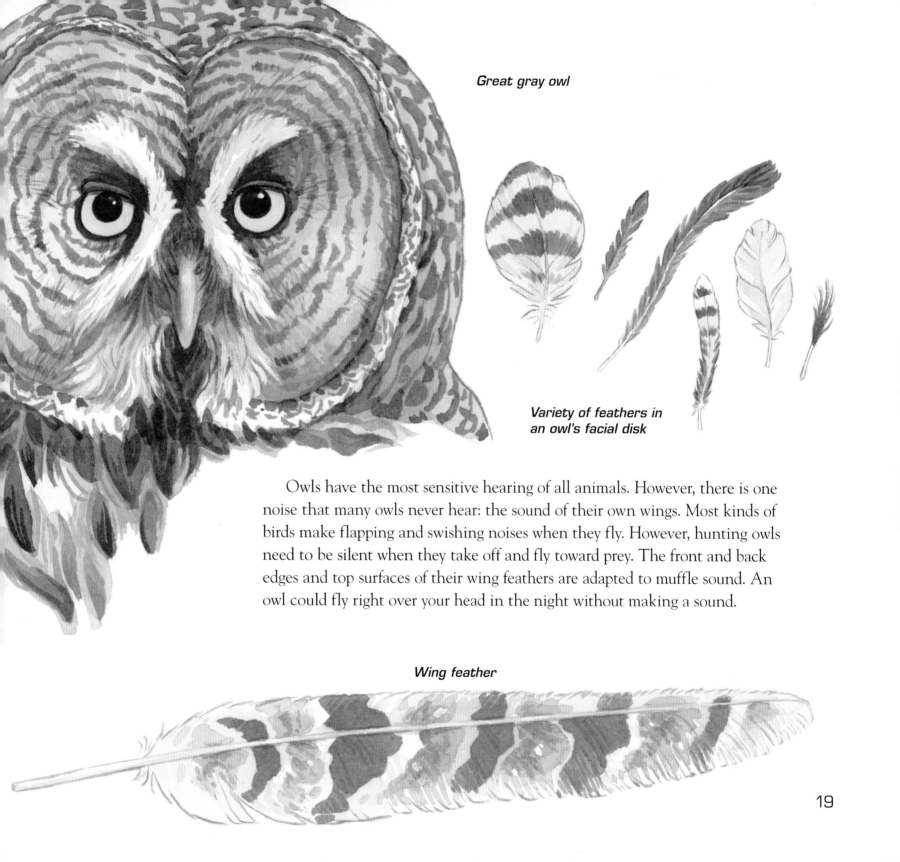

Great gray owl

Variety of feathers in an owl's facial disk

Owls have the most sensitive hearing of all animals. However, there is one noise that many owls never hear: the sound of their own wings. Most kinds of birds make flapping and swishing noises when they fly. However, hunting owls need to be silent when they take off and fly toward prey. The front and back edges and top surfaces of their wing feathers are adapted to muffle sound. An owl could fly right over your head in the night without making a sound.

Wing feather

19

Great horned owl

All owls are **predators**, which means that they kill and eat other animals. An owl hunting at night needs to use both its keen eyesight and its super-sensitive hearing. Imagine an owl as it sits and waits on a tree branch in the woods. The owl watches for any movement, listens for any sound. Hundreds of feet away, a mouse scurries among dead leaves. The owl instantly turns its head toward the tiny sound. Another rustle in the leaves. The owl moves its head slightly, pinpointing the exact location of the hidden mouse.

The mouse steps on a dry leaf and makes another tiny noise. The owl launches into the air. With its silent flight, the owl can still hear the mouse if it moves again. Getting close, the owl stops beating its wings and glides straight toward its prey. Suddenly, it moves its head back and thrusts its feet forward. Its toes spread apart, then its **talons** (claws) seize the mouse. The owl's talons or beak kill the mouse, and soon it is swallowed, headfirst.

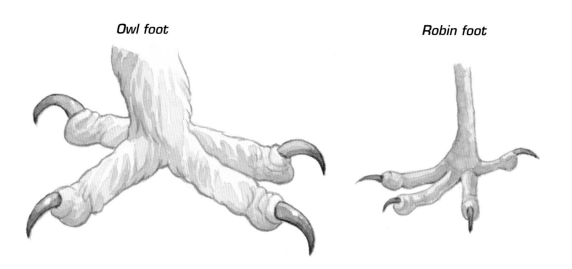

Owl foot   *Robin foot*

Birds have four toes on each foot. Most species, including chickens, crows, and songbirds, have three toes in front and one at the back of each foot. A few groups of birds, including parrots, woodpeckers, and owls, have a different kind of foot: two toes always face forward, one always faces back, and the fourth toe can turn toward the front or back. When an owl pounces on prey, it turns its fourth toe back so that two toes are facing forward and two are facing back. The toes and talons catch the animal, gripping it tightly. This type of foot also helps fishing owls hold onto their slippery prey.

Saw-whet owl regurgitating pellet

Screech owl

An owl usually carries small prey in one foot as it flies to a safe eating place. With larger prey, the owl stays put and uses its sharp beak to tear the animal apart. It gulps the pieces down. Everything is swallowed—not just muscles and organs, but bones, claws, feathers, and fur.

Owls digest their food differently from most other birds. In many birds, swallowed food goes first to a **crop**—a pouch where food is stored. Later it can be digested by the bird, or spit up to feed young. Owls have no crops. Their swallowed food goes straight to their stomachs, where digestion begins. Then it reaches the **gizzard**, a muscular organ where the food is churned and digested further. But the digestive fluids of owls are not as strong as those of many other birds. This means that more feathers, fur, bones, and other hard-to-digest parts remain intact in the gizzard. The muscles of the gizzard pack the undigested material into a pellet, which then moves back up the digestive track. Finally, at least six hours after eating, the owl throws up, or **regurgitates**, a pellet.

Once rid of a pellet, the owl can eat again. So, once or twice a day, a pellet falls to the ground beneath an owl's roosting place. Pellets are shaped like little sausages. Those from big owls can be three inches long. These little packages are gifts to ornithologists and students who want to know what owls eat. With some knowledge of animal skeletons, they can examine the skulls, bones, beaks, and other items in a pellet to identify the kinds of birds and mammals the owl recently ate.

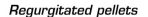

Regurgitated pellets

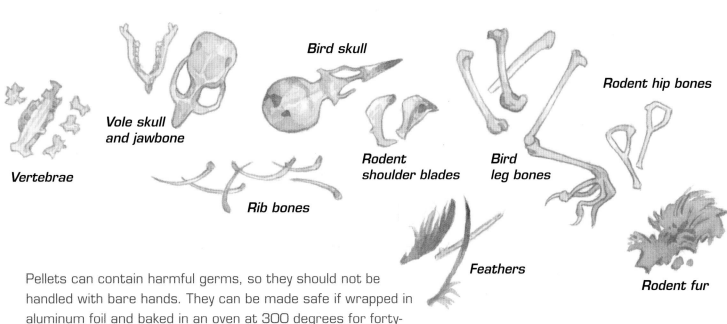

Little owl

Short-eared owl

Barn owl

Snowy owl

Vertebrae

Vole skull and jawbone

Rib bones

Bird skull

Rodent shoulder blades

Bird leg bones

Rodent hip bones

Feathers

Rodent fur

Pellets can contain harmful germs, so they should not be handled with bare hands. They can be made safe if wrapped in aluminum foil and baked in an oven at 300 degrees for forty-five minutes. Also, there are science supply companies that sell treated pellets free from dangerous germs.

During mating season, male and female owls give special calls or make other sounds to find one another. To impress a female, a male short-eared owl may display his flying skills with a "sky dance"—flying high, diving, clapping his wings together. He may also show off to a female on the ground by parading, strutting, and fluttering his feathers. A male has other ways to impress a female, such as giving special gifts of freshly killed mice, lemmings, scorpions, fish, or other prey, depending on the owl species.

Female owls choose the nest site, but owls do not build nests. The biggest species often use nests, made of branches and twigs, that were built by other birds, including hawks and crows. In the West, long-eared owls like to use nests built by magpies. Holes created by woodpeckers in trees and cacti are just right for elf owls. In the flat Arctic tundra, snowy owls pick a spot on the ground, usually on a high mound that offers a view of the surroundings.

The abundance of food in the months *before* nesting affects how many eggs a female can lay. Before the female lays eggs, she stops hunting, and the male brings her food. The number of young that survive depends on the amount of food the male can catch and bring to the nest. For example, when lemmings are scarce, a snowy owl might lay two to three eggs. When there are plenty of lemmings, she might lay eight to ten eggs. Whatever the number, she keeps them warm, day and night, and only leaves the nest for short breaks.

Great gray owls

25

A mother owl lays a new egg about every two to three days. To hatch, each egg needs about four weeks of warmth from her body. A baby owl (**owlet**) chips itself free of its shell with a sharp **egg tooth** on the tip of its beak. Since the eggs aren't laid all at once, the owlets hatch at different times. The first egg laid hatches first. If a nest has six eggs, the sixth owlet hatches after the first one has already been growing for ten or more days. If food is scarce, the smallest nestlings may die. When food is plentiful, big owlets are fed well before the mother feeds her smaller nestlings.

Snowy owls

26

Screech owlets branching

Just-hatched owlets are helpless and don't open their eyes for several days. They are covered with fluffy down. At first, their mother gathers them close under her body and wings to keep them warm. If the owlets are well-fed, they grow fast. Once they gain some body fat, they can keep themselves warm. This frees their mother. She joins her mate—hunting, hunting, hunting—to feed their ever-hungry young.

Within a few weeks, the owlets lose their downy feathers, which are gradually replaced by other feathers. They still can't fly, but begin to explore beyond home. This is called **branching**, because owlets in tree nests hop about on nearby branches. Owlets on the ground also venture out from their nest. Branching owlets flap their wings, grow stronger, and get ready for their first flight.

Tawny owl of Eurasia

28

An owl's first year is full of peril. Some young owls die of starvation. They fly out into an unfamiliar world, and at first are not skillful at catching food. They try to hunt, but also keep making begging calls to their parents. Their parents do help, but usually stop when the young are ready to live independently.

The young must also learn how to avoid becoming food themselves. They may be hunted by foxes, badgers, hawks, and other predators—including other species of owls. Cars and trucks can be especially deadly for owls. The grassy, weedy open spaces alongside roads are good habitats for rodents, rabbits, and other prey. Some kinds of owls hunt there. When an owl flies—its vision and hearing focused on a mouse—it may not notice an oncoming car.

Young or old, owls can be wiped out if their habitat is destroyed. This is the greatest threat to owls worldwide. About half of the world's owls live only in older forests, with many big trees. Vast areas of such forests have been cut down, and more are cut each day. This threatens the survival of forest owls, especially in South America and Asia, including the Philippines. Ground-nesting owls also lose their living places. In Canada and the United States, the open land habitat of burrowing owls and short-eared owls shrinks as it is replaced by cropland, housing, and other land developments.

Owls also may die when people try to control mice and other pests with poisons. Before the pests die, owls catch and eat some of this poisoned prey. As a result, humans kill the very birds that can help control pests! Some farmers value barn owls because they know these owls kill many grain-eating mice. In the Netherlands, farmers try to attract these owls by building special openings and nesting places in their barns.

Barred owl

All over the world, there are still people who fear owls, and sometimes kill them. However, growing numbers of people have moved beyond old myths and superstitions. They know that owls are harmless to people. In books, schools, science museums, nature centers, and on websites, we can learn the truth about owls. Real owls are much more appealing than imaginary ones.

People who appreciate owls try to save forests and other owl habitats. Even preserving dead trees can be helpful, since forest owls often roost or nest in the hollows of such trees. In some places, people build nest boxes for screech owls and others that may lack natural nesting sites.

Instead of fearing owls, many people are delighted to hear one call. They are thrilled to know that such a fascinating wild bird is nearby. Actually seeing one is something to celebrate. Many agree with words written in 1854 by American philosopher Henry David Thoreau: "I rejoice that there are owls."

Glossary

binocular vision—The ability to see in three dimensions. This happens when the view from two forward-facing eyes overlaps. Binocular eyesight helps the viewer judge distances accurately. Many birds, including ducks, have eyes on the sides of their heads, so the views from their two eyes do not overlap. They have monocular, or flat, two-dimensional vision.

branching—Exploratory behavior of flightless young owls as they leave their nest and clamber among nearby tree branches or other surroundings.

crop—The upper part of a bird's digestive system where swallowed food is stored and partly digested.

egg tooth—A hard spur that every kind of unhatched young bird has on the tip of its beak, which helps it break out of its egg. It drops off within a week or two after the hatchling is free of its egg.

facial disk—The flat or saucer-shaped surface of an owl's face. Several kinds of feathers make up the disk, which is a key part of an owl's sense of hearing. Sounds are reflected from the feathers of the disk to the owl's ears.

gizzard—A muscular pouch in a bird's digestive system where food is churned, mixed, and partly digested.

habitat—The place or environment where an organism normally lives. For example, the usual habitat of snowy owls is the vast open space of the Arctic tundra.

ornithologists—Scientists who study birds.

owlet—A baby owl, after hatching from its egg. Note: there are several species of pygmy owls, from Asia and Africa, which are called owlets as adults. They include the Asian barred owlet and the jungle owlet.

predators—Animals that kill and eat other animals.

regurgitate—To bring up undigested food from the digestive system and spit it out of the mouth. For owls and some other species of birds, the regurgitated parts of prey are called pellets.

scops owls—Species of mostly small owls that scientists once classified in the same group (*Otus*) as the screech owls of the Americas. Screech owls are now considered different enough to be in a separate classification (*Megascops*). Scops owls live in Europe, Africa, and Asia.

talons—Sharp, curved claws on the toes of owls, hawks, eagles, and other predatory birds.

tundra—An Arctic habitat of low-growing plants, including mosses, lichens, grasses, sedges, and dwarf shrubs. It has long winters of extreme cold and no sunlight, and short, two-month summers when the sun never sets.

vertebrae—A column of bones that fit together to form an animal's backbone, or spine, which begins at the base of the skull.

voles—Small rodents, related to mice, that have small eyes and ears, and short tails. Species include the prairie vole and the meadow vole. Voles are *not* related to small, burrowing mammals called moles.

To Learn More

Books and periodicals

Brower, Kenneth. "The Proof Is in the Pellet." *Audubon*, March 2004, 78–83.

Chandler, David. *Barn Owl*. Buffalo, NY: Firefly, 2011.

Esbensen, Barbara J. *Tiger with Wings: The Great Horned Owl*. New York: Orchard, 1991.

Gish, Melissa. *Owls: Living Wild*. Mankato, MN: Creative Education, 2012.

Hammerslough, Jane. *Owl Puke*. New York: Workman, 2004.

Hiscock, Bruce. *Ookpik: The Travels of a Snowy Owl*. Honesdale, PA: Boyds Mills Press, 2008.

Markle, Sandra. *Owls*. Minneapolis, MN: Carolrhoda, 2004.

Richardson, Adele. *Owls: Flat-Faced Flyers*. Minneapolis, MN: Capstone, 2003.

Sattler, Helen Roney. *The Book of North American Owls*. New York: Clarion, 1995.

Warhol, Tom. *Owls*. New York: Benchmark, 2004.

Websites *

www.allaboutbirds.org

The Cornell Lab of Ornithology offers information, photos, and owl call recordings of North American species.

www.arkive.org

The ARKive Organization offers information, photos, owl call recordings, and videos of many species.

www.owlpages.com

This site is rich with information, a photo gallery, and an owl sounds gallery of species from all over the world.

*active at time of publication

Sources

The main sources of information for this book include the following books and periodicals, several written by owl researchers:

Angier, Natalie. "The Owl Comes Into Its Own." *New York Times*, Feb. 25, 2013, 1.

Backhouse, Frances. *Owls of North America*. Buffalo, NY: Firefly, 2008.

Duncan, James. *Owls of the World: Their Lives, Behavior and Survival*. Buffalo, NY: Firefly, 2003.

Duncan, James. *The Complete Book of North American Owls*. San Diego, CA: Thunder Bay Press, 2013.

Johnsgard, Paul. *North American Owls: Biology and Natural History*. Washington, D.C.: Smithsonian Institution Press, 2002.

Long, Kim. *Owls: A Wildlife Handbook*. Boulder, CO: Johnson Books, 1998.

Lynch, Wayne. *Owls of the United States and Canada: A Complete Guide to Their Biology and Behavior*. Baltimore, MD: Johns Hopkins University Press, 2007.

Taylor, Marianne. *Owls*. Ithaca, NY: Cornell University Press, 2012.

Tekiela, Stan. *Intriguing Owls: Extraordinary Images and Insight*. Cambridge, MN: Adventure Publications, 2009.

Index